North End Love Songs

NORTH END LOVE SONGS

Katherena Vermette

The
Muses'
Company

North End Love Songs
first published 2012 by The Muses' Company
An imprint of J. Gordon Shillingford Publishing Inc.
©2012 Katherena Vermette
Reprinted September 2014

The Muses' Company Series Editor: Clarise Foster
Cover design by Terry Gallagher/Doowah Design Inc.
Interior design by Relish New Brand Experience, Inc.
Author photo by Rosanna Deerchild
Cover art by Reuben Boulette
Printed and bound in Canada on 100% post-consumer
recycled paper.

We acknowledge the financial support of the Manitoba
Arts Council and The Canada Council for the Arts for our
publishing program.

LIBRARY AND ARCHIVES CANADA CATALOGUING IN PUBLICATION

Vermette, Katherena, 1977-
     North End love songs / Katherena Vermette.

Poems.
ISBN 978-1-897289-76-1

     I. Title.

PS8643.E74N67 2012   C811'.6   C2012-905047

J. GORDON SHILLINGFORD PUBLISHING
P.O. BOX 86, RPO CORYDON AVENUE
WINNIPEG, MB CANADA R3M 3S3

For Ela and Rowan

Also dedicated to the memory of my brother,
Donovan Wayne Attley 1972–1991

Table of Contents

A tough life needs a tough language—and that is what poetry is. That is what literature offers—a language powerful enough to say how it is.

—JEANETTE WINTERSON

POISED FOR FLIGHT

A cuckoo's cry:
and today—just today—
there is nobody by.

—SHOHAKU

selkirk avenue

1

thrush

girl walks up
selkirk avenue
head down
body huddled
into herself
shakes with winter
squeezes
her arms around
an oversized
grey sweater
as if she could
hide and not feel
the cold

2

robin

girl stands on
selkirk avenue
head down
her body cries
like a baby alone
paces
a round circle way
too young body squeezed
into too tight clothing
breathes out
with her whole chest
puffed out bright
and red
as if she's
beautiful
as if she's
proud

hummingbird

girl drives down
selkirk avenue
looks forward
as if she don't
look at all of them
they won't be there
doors locked
too loud music
drowns all the voices
outside
like her windows
are only tv screens
and the other girls
on the street
are only a show

pritchard park

she sits
on the far park bench
exhales cigarette smoke
and cold
her fingers trace
the rough
lines others have carved
into the wood

her youngest daughter calls
wants to swing
wants to be pushed
until her feet kick the sky
until her little face hurts
from wind
and laughter

she stubs out
her half finished smoke
stumbles toward
the play structure

where her oldest daughter thumps
her boots across the frozen
play bridge
she likes the sound
how its hinges
have a special song
in winter

all the pretty birds
a poem in many voices

magpie

magpie likes to
collect
she covets
hoards
keeps:

when she is fifteen
she finds beers like
shiny treasures
wants them
drinks like practice
and soon can drink her uncles
under the table
or so they like to tell her
but beer don't grow on trees
or so they like to tell her
when she is sixteen
she finds glimmering
heroin but that
costs even more
than beer

Katherena Vermette/17

sparrow

sparrow so small
bones can break
with the gentlest
touch:

when she is fourteen
and her cousin eighteen
he buys her first bottle
vodka it is
so strong
she sips quick
and soon can barely move
he seems cool
his lips drip sweetness
his hands drift across
her body like promises
when he pushes away
she covers herself with
discarded clothing
he laughs says

don't worry
your mom's really your aunty so
there's no real blood between us

shrike

shrike loves wind
dives into it bravely
shakes her feathers
until they are plump
down around her
protect her:

when she is twelve
Shane steals a cigarette
from his mom
and they hide up in his room
being super quiet
window wide
open to winter
they lean into it
suck back smoke
he says

I really like you, you know

her eyes turn up to see him
only like? she asks

he laughs and says
here, let me show you

Katherena Vermette/19

chickadee

chickadee loves sun
sits in it all summer
singing the song
that is
her name:

when she's thirteen
she stays at her granny's
for a summer
the house has a long
screened in porch
that smells like
spilt beer and old people
the floor crunches
with sunflower seed shells

an old man hangs out there
watches the sun
through the screen

when she meets him
he looks her up and down
and up again

well he sighs through
toothless gums
you must be your mother's

finch

finch feels like flannel
looks rough with
feathers missing
crooked legs
dark with weather
she is broken
like a shell:

when the girl is four
and still lives with
her mom
her mom has parties

she sleeps in
the small room
with her brother
it's her job
to give
him his bottle
if he wakes up

she keeps it
on the window sill
but one night
it's so hot
the milk sours

so she has to
open the door
let in the sound
and light
walk through
the people

Katherena Vermette/21

all the way
to the fridge

she can't find her mom
but her auntie
hugs her
like she's so excited
to see her
helps her
pour new milk
and pushes her back
through the living room

she watches
the faces blur
as she goes
familiar
but different
smudged somehow

for a long time
she thinks
all grownups change
like that

on those long nights
she stays awake
listening to the music
the laughter
the yelling

stays awake
waiting
for her brother to cry
but if anyone comes in

to their small room
she pretends
to be
asleep

Katherena Vermette/23

egg

she is waiting
she is
a swollen belly
housed in soft bones
waiting
wrapped in glowing skin
waiting
a child in june
waiting
an infant
an egg
waiting
for just the perfect
moment
to crack

blackbird

a baby's cry
rises into the infinite
night
unanswered

below
voices dissolve
into desperate
bass cheap
rhythms

below
words are lost
to the din

but from this distance
her cry is clear
resonates into low
clouds
finds its
pitch
against the stars

already
she is strong
already
she is

a
ca
pel
la

Katherena Vermette/25

blue jay

poised for flight
one small foot
on the curb
like a sprinter
this girl
with such rough skin
the colour of concrete
in the rain
this girl
is ready
to fly

her eyes pierce
the wind pulls ,
her hair back
like a mother's hand
making a ponytail
she looks
for a break

falls into
a clumsy run
dodges cars with more
luck than precision
lands triumphant
on the other side

pushes the open
sides of her windbreaker
together
and falls behind
a thin line of orange
patrols just leaving
their posts

not far off
a school bell rings

Katherena Vermette/27

go

one evening
her eyes
will gaze up
into the pink
of a darkening sky
and she will
raise her arms
like a lark
to the wind while
the trees wave
her on

and she will just
let go

redbird

she dances
in long red cloth
with gold rings sewn
into lines across her body
she curves
a round circle way
jingling
gently to the drum
her hair
bouncing black feathers
her dress
wide red wings
her lithe feet
so light
no one
would be surprised
if she really did
take flight

Katherena Vermette/29

happy girls

two
drunk
girls on a bridge
their long hair
cuts the wind
under a winter sky
ready to burst

too
drunk
girls pause
in one moment
of a cruel
white
night

one
girl burrows
into her thin jacket
emerges with
a fully lit
smoke

one
girl leans
her belly into
the cold cement rail
reaches over the river
for the first
flake
of snow

parkgrrl

she runs barefoot
in the park
hair in her face
brushed aside
with a quick
chubby palm

daylight dances
on her pure
dark skin
as she rattles off verses
buries caterpillars
in the sand
calls weeds
flowers

she would
stay there
forever

make the teeter totter
her dinner table
cuddle up to sleep
on a swing
and sing lullabies
to bugs
as the sun goes down

when she wakes
she would have only to
kick her legs
to the pale clouds
and breathe
a breakfast
of morning sun

yellowbird

she loves yellow
has yellow days
is going through
a yellow period
but unlike artists
she is never unhappy

she loves the heat
welcomes each
summer day
like a guest
to our house

believes
it's her job
to pick the dandelions
a gentle massacre
she is
a golden head
in a sea of honey
likes how
they stay so yellow
even when
they are dead

trains

lights over the train yard
tumble out toward
the ground
a ramble of stars
a makeshift
constellation

she can see it
from her yard
as she smokes
another cigarette

her daughters think
those lights are stars
that touch all the way
down to earth
and the trains are just
funny farting cars
bumping together
in the night

listening
in their beds
as the trains
sigh and audibly change
they hear
every sound
and still
sleep

still awake
she listens
and smokes
another cigarette

treegrrl

she wants to   .
open her arms
wide enough
stretch them out
like an elm's long branches
to catch
a thousand birds
and hold them close

she thinks
all the animals at the zoo
belong to her
knows them through
her thin tan skin
greets the lion
like an old friend
nods to the monkeys
like cousins

she knows
how we all share
the same air

brownbird

grass isn't even
green yet
her brown face
turns up
toward the sun
like a flower

she runs
into its thick shine
her legs thin shadows
over pale grass
over puddles
without hesitation
she glides
just above
the earth

brown hair curling out
into chaos
cheeks red
with breath
small eyes so deep
distracted

she runs
she never looks
back

swinging lessons

push forward
from your core
right down
to your belly
hang on
to these chains
don't let go
even if your hands get sweaty
stretch your legs
out in front of you
as you go forward
bend them down
as you swing back
keep going

keep your legs moving
like you're running
like you're trying
to catapult yourself
into the sky
until you can only feel
wind all around you
until you look up
and all you see is
thin summer clouds
strong bright sun
and all the tree tops
dancing

cedar wax wing

a bird lies
in the middle
of the sidewalk
perfect
but dead
it has a black mask
over its eyes
like a bandit
a tuft of dark hair
on its head
like a Mohawk
and a shiny grey body
not unlike silver
resplendent
like a jewel

the bird is called
cedar wax wing
the anishnaabe name it
zegibanooji
and give it
a place of honour
in their stories
though no one can
tell her
why

NORTENDLUVSONG

i thank You God for most this amazing
day: for the leaping greenly spirits of trees
and a blue true dream of sky; and for everything
which is natural which is infinite which is yes

—E.E. CUMMINGS

bannerman avenue

1

girl looks down
bannerman avenue
elms tower
branches overhead
interlaced like fingers
cup around her
hold her in

grey street goes
bone straight
right under
fingers making a steeple
a church adorned

black leaves
across pavement

branches wave
in the sun

2

girls walk
right down
the middle of
bannerman avenue
too important
to be ushered off
to the sidewalk
sway narrow hips
to let cars pass
spit over shoulders
their bodies tough
used and
innocent

3

she likes to
balance
on the curb
as they go
one foot in front
of the other
hands out
as far as they can
reach
steps over
broken cement
kicks debris aside
arms all the way
out

she watches
her steps
and the leaves
dance shadows
across her
upturned palms

seed

in the spring
she watches
tree born seeds
set to sky
like birds
embryonic leaves
with translucent skin
so light
they can rest on
the warm air
and meander down
unseen paths
to earth

window

she lies
on her small square yard
looks up
to the sky

there's no elm tree
in front of her house
a space made
a window
in the long
archway

watches
clouds pass

imagines
all the things
they could
be

dust

it's her job to dust
the dining room
the long wood table
the high plate rail
has to stand
on a chair
run the rag down
the length of wood
her finger in the crease
where the plate edge
is supposed to go

but there are no plates
her mother prefers
knick nacks
native inspired
stuff like
the pictures of her children
framed in fake gold
between a soap stone carving
and a small painting
of a child with perfect
all the way brown skin
resplendent in regalia
and eagle feathers

Guy

she pulls her bike
between houses
bumps it over old stones
if she stretches out her arms
one hand touching
the white siding of her house
the other flat
on Guy's

his bathroom
next to her bedroom
so she can
hear the water
when he takes a bath

hear him cry out
when his dad
throws him
against a wall
feel her window shake

once she let him
borrow her bike
he took it to
st. john's park
to ride in the ditches
by the river
and he brought it back
all muddy
but she didn't say anything

when he shows up
at school all bruised
tells everyone
how he got jumped

she just nods
like everyone else

summer

in summer the elms
gentle
thick
intertwined
block out sun

the nortend is
houses all different
shades of snow
chipped paint trim
boxing windows
bedsheets
hung inside

some with
fake brick siding
rough as sandpaper
shingles stapled
over rotting wood

winter

in winter the elms
black
skeletons

sky a white cloud
breaking open

windows translucent
with wrinkled plastic

torn
where small children
pick holes
so they can
look outside

merry christmas

these houses are tired
sighing
like old ladies
bent over themselves
in the cold

eavestroughs frown
christmas lights flicker
like costume jewelry
behind broken windows
and toys forgotten
in the snow

family

elms around us
like aunties
uncles
cousins
all different
but with the same skin

the tall one with
thinning foliage
sticking straight up
branches scratching
at the sky

the wide one
split in two
half way up
looks like scissors
or two legs
bent and kicking

the gnarled one with
warts all over its face

the one with
the swirled branch
curved out over
cathedral avenue
looped like hair
around a finger

but her favourites
are the ones by the river
they spread low
and stay close
to the earth

those ones she can
climb into
lean against
the strong dark bark
rest her small body
within their round arms

their sharp leaves
reach out over the river

she watches how
the waves fold
into each other
like family

peanut park

the girls know
the playstructure
at peanut park is old
they can count its years
by the history
cut into it

its top
like a fort
they sink inside
shadows thick
and clammy
where no one can see them
if they want to smoke

the walls with
names
dates
hearts
swears burned
into the wood
runes from
a different age

they read them
out loud
wonder about
who made them
if they too sat here
passing around
a single
cigarette

big gulps

1

girls walk back down
bannerman avenue
sip big gulps
talk too loud

elms curve
above them
like a roof

the nortend is always quiet
during the day

2

girls sit on
church steps
sipping big gulps

every flavour
but diet
in hers
a delicate
chemistry
she shares
in small sips
but never tells
her whole secret

girls share cigarettes
small bags of chips
sometimes
a stolen can of beer
and stories
of their short lives
how many boyfriends
they'd had
already
how many times they
had to

four of them
on the church steps
talk 'til after
the sun goes down
cups empty
fingers licked
of chip salt

wildflowers

it's the wildflowers
she feels sorry for
they've got to
watch their backs
nobody wants
them around
people spread poison
to kill them off
call them weeds

she thinks
it's a shame 'cause
if you let them
just grow
they're really quite
beautiful
flowering pink
butter yellow
can fill a dark space with
splendid green
if you let them

but if they flower
they'll seed
if you let them
they'll take over
choke out all those
poppies and marigolds
roses and daffodils
no planted flower
stands a chance
against a pack of weeds

so they get yanked
roots burned
concrete's thrown
over them

still they sprout
all over the place
push through
cracks in the sidewalks
congregate on otherwise
respectable lawns

darn squatters
she thinks
they really gotta
watch their backs

nortendluvsong

her house has
a large veranda
off the back
an addition
like an afterthought
the roof flat
like a balcony
just under
her bedroom window

sometimes she
unhooks the screen
sits out on
the grey shingles
listens to the cars pass on
salter street
loud tvs in nearby houses
dogs bark
sirens wail
get close
fade away

in the room
next to hers
her brother plays
heavy metal
the sound muffled
far away
inside his loud music
gets into everything
but out here
it is almost soundless
soft
as a love song

Katherena Vermette/59

ghosts

ghosts in the basement
long lonely
creatures
set into shadows

deep holes
of the stone
walls

if she has to
go down there
she turns on
all the lights
and races up
as fast as she can

after her brother died
her stepfather would
sit there
in the dark
smoke
export a cigarettes
talk to his son
and all the other
damp shadows

she managed to avoid

Wayne

she forgot her keys
and had to knock
at the living room window
her brother pulls
up the blind
points at the clock
laughs

let me in she begs

her feet cold
her friends
as gone
as her curfew
he slowly lowers
the blind
turns up the tv

she could only
wait
sit in the old
orange armchair
her favourite
of the discarded
porch furniture

after he died
and the world twisted
like a rag rung out
of water
she would sit
out there
smoking
cross legged
on the porch table

the old one that used to be
in the house
and thought
the world couldn't possibly
change
anymore

when he
finally tires of his game
and she hears him
unlock the door

he doesn't say
anything
just goes back
to watching tv

green disease

"My words are nothing. Hear the leaves."
—URSULA K. LEGUIN

she watches the city
cut down trees
bright orange
X
a kill mark
spray painted
across the bark

they come in
an over sized white truck
stretch out a long metal arm
with a large bucket
at the end
a man gets in
rises up off the street
like an elevator
or hot air balloon

with a loud buzzing saw
he starts at the top
cuts the leafy branches
sways gently
back and forth
as if carving a sculpture
or trimming hair

branches fall
lightly to the earth
where other men
absentmindedly
gather them
into a pile

Katherena Vermette/63

she watches
until the tree looks nothing
like itself
it is naked
bald
amputated

the bucket lowers slightly
the trunk stabbed
the man cuts a short
thick piece
until it loosens
and falls heavy

cut after cut
until the tree is barely
taller than the grass
and pieces sit around
the stump
like stones

when the men leave
she studies
the pieces of the tree
tries to count
the yellow rings that were once
inside

but each blond circle blurs
into the next

under a shroud of trees

she is with a boy
in the heavy
summer rain
they are dry
under a shroud of trees

impossible elms
so intertwined
the concrete
underneath
barely changes colour

where the boy
leans her against
the soft bark
cups his palms
to her cheeks

they stand there
holding
each other
the thunder rumbling
through the trees
through their bones

until it stops
as suddenly as it
started
and sky breaks bright
through clouds

Katherena Vermette/65

he takes her hand
they run through
puddles
across the nortend
they chase
sun

NOVEMBER

Woke up to the sound of pouring rain
The wind would whisper and I'd think of you

—SKID ROW

picture

1

in the front hallway
his sister watches
him tie his shoes
a foot propped
up on the small stool

he wears jeans
the colour of snow
a jacket blue and thin
even though it is
such a cold
november

he wears a black
concert t shirt
bright writing with
an eagle clutching
a large peace sign
in its claws

2

he tosses and feathers
his soft black hair
with thin brown hands
checks his reflection
in the mirror

his sister asks him
to borrow a sweater
he hesitates
teases
finally says
fine

he turns at the door
smirks
waves
the wind pushes
his hair over his face
and he's gone

3

her mother picks
several pictures
to put in the newspaper
different ones showing
different things
multiple profiles

but the newspaper takes
the one with
his hat hung low
half his face
in shadow

the headline reads:
Native Man Missing After Binge

she cuts it out
folds it in two
puts it in
a photo album

she thinks he would like
that they called him
a Man

4

they make
posters
with a picture of him
holding the teddy bear
her mother bought
last christmas
he poses
reluctant
bored
his smile thin
christmas tree reticent
in the faded
background

the poster's thick
writing in black
marker

last seen

wearing

if seen

contact

friends

her friends sit
at her living room
window
curtain pushed
aside
to watch her brother
get into a car
they gawk in their
young girl way

they are
a lot younger than
they think they are
they giggle

she watches
indifferent

lost

her brother is missing
like a glove
or a sock
a set of keys
gone

his room empty
the sheen on his posters
dull from lack of light
curtains closed

her brother is now
a picture
stuck to a tree
a light post
on tv once

he could be
lying on a road
in a field
in the river
maybe
lost
in the snow
in nothing
but his thin
jacket
his bare
hands

record

1

when it's too cold
to go outside
they sit on
the sagging futon
in her living room

blinds pulled up
so they can
watch the street

they record
videos off
the music channel
have special vhs tapes
for different kinds
of music

they have to be quick
to get the timing right
push off
push on

2

they watch videos
until the tapes
wear thin
and start to skip

the girls warm their hands
on teenage drama
he's dating who?
she said what?

such a cold november
nothing melted
not even a bit

they sit around
waiting

she wears
her brother's sweater
and is really good
at recording
videos

she knows the half
second delay
how to hit the button
just in time
on

heavy metal ballads

1

her brother ripped
the stickers off
his vhs tapes
wrote W
for Wayne
in thick black marker
on the black plastic
you couldn't see
unless you tilted it
to the light

he taped
rocker videos
heavy metal
screaming guitars
head banging music

she only likes the ballads
tough guys with long hair
and hard faces
singing
love
loss
tears
in short
4 minutes
segments

mixed tape

side a:

1. 18 and Life

her friend takes her to
the guidance counselor
she doesn't see the point
but her friend won't go
without her

2. Patience

the dining room table
stacked with papers
her brother's face
on all of them
like labels
on cans of soup

3. Long Cold Winter

his football team
organizes a search party
scruffy boys in
orange jerseys climb
snow banks
along the river
north
all the way to
lockport

4. Without You

she is as still as silence
jolts every time
the phone rings

5. More than Words

the family sliced into wedges
like pie

6. Don't Know What You Got

the cold
wet
quiet
when
everyone else
leaves

side b:

7. Nothing Else Matters

the family goes to two psychics
and an elder

8. Every Rose has Its Thorn

one says he will call soon
one says he is dead

one says he is
traveling
north

9. What You Give

words
evaporate
condense
in the air

drip
down
walls

10. Don't Cry

her stepfather
tells everyone
his son is
dead

and he isn't going to look
anymore

11. Home Sweet Home

her mother moves
wide and slow
almost imperceptible
limbs floating
as if in water

12. November Rain

the girl walks under
winter naked elms
such a cold november
a season warmer
than her house

christmas

her mother and stepfather
want to
look at pictures
remember

the good times
they call them
as they pull her
into the living room

she wants to
be anywhere else

slips out the door
with fluid
silent movements
runs down
the street
along parked cars

just in case
she has to duck

makes it
to her friend's
sits with them
eats chips
spits sunflower seeds
into an empty
big gulp cup

her mother shows up
within half an hour
no one lies well enough
to keep her out

the girl hides
in the closet
coats brush
the top of her head
her mother finds her

she is so
angry
but they are
silent
all the way
home

new years

the girls decide
to throw a new year's party
pour chips into bowls
she brings vhs tapes
the ones with
the good dance music

they spill balloons
into a toy net
and string it up
above their heads
to be released
at midnight

they dance
all wear
kookaburra sweaters
in different colours
laugh
tell stories
he did what?
she's dating who?

someone's boyfriend
bumps into the string
and all the balloons
tumble out
he says sorry with
shrugged shoulders

they all laugh
wish each other
happy new year
even though
it's only 9:30 pm

almost instantly

1 .

when a person
is drunk
in the bitter
freezing
winter
all their blood
rushes
to the surface
of their skin

they get
dizzy

disorient
almost instantly

2

river currents
speed in opposing
directions
on the surface
it looks like goes
south but
just a few feet under
water whips north

the pull between
the two
so strong
it can break bones
it can pull a person

down
almost instantly

in winter when

in winter when
you can barely tell
where the ground
ends
and the river
begins

in the winter when
snow covers earth
and it all looks
the same

spring

they all wait
her brother's missing
posters tossed
across the nortend
oversized confetti
tacked to elm trees
taped to light posts

his life
indistinguishable
from other information
stuck
in public places
paper worn
by weather
loose at the corners
torn
from staples
whipping in the wind

Katherena Vermette/87

found

they find him
they say
dental records
no need to see

she imagines
her brother's body
swelled

like hers
pushed all the way
to the edge
unidentifiable

they think
he tried
to walk across the river
in a cold november when
it was almost frozen

just not
all the way

the end

she walks
in bright spring
colours
the may sun
shining tiny
increments through
the low curve of elms

she walks
the length of the street
from the end
all the way to the river
where the concrete
starts

then she turns
around
and walks
the three slow
blocks
to her house

Katherena Vermette/89

indians

indians go missing
they tell the family
indians go missing
everyday
blue suits shrug
no sense looking
they said
he'll turn up when
he gets bored
or broke

indians drown
the family finds out
happens everyday
this land floods
with dead indians
this river swells
freezes
breaks open
cold arms of ice
welcomes indians

indians get drunk
don't we know it?
do stupid things
like being young
like going home alone
like walking across
a frozen river
not quite frozen
and not making it
to the other side

heavy metal ballads

2

her brother is beautiful
hair brushed gently
across shoulders
like newly born
bird feathers
so soft but
the downy black
could never be
touched

he is tight jeans
concert t shirt
and smirks practiced
in front of mirrors
perfected to cover
every silver tooth

her brother is
heavy metal ballads
a thin ripple bass line
a long
slow current
of guitar
a smooth
wave of lyrics

you always
remember

Katherena Vermette/91

picture

for donovan

8

dirty face smiles
diaper hangs
to dark knees
caked with mud
almost the same
colour as
his sun kissed cheeks
kissed a lot
this wild baby
happy in the grass
paused for a breath
and a picture
now as ruddy
as the child in it
edges frayed from being
pocketed too long
colours faded
absentminded
folds marks
make a trail
over his feet
erase
his toes

things she does the day before the wake

picks out a dress
a long one
to hide her thighs
floral not black

sits in the big orange chair
with legs hugged
into her chest
watches night come
streetlights turn on
slowly

writes a short
rhyming poem
that starts with the lines:
shed a tear for days passed by
for all the times now gone
starts every line with
shed a tear
prints it out
slowly
in pencil
erases
and fixes until
the paper is soft
with rubbing

gets a phone call
from a boy her friend likes
a boy from her brother's school
he offers
his condolences
he calls them
when he asks her

what she is doing saturday
she tells him
I don't know

comforts a doubly
devastated friend

makes a mixed tape of
heavy metal ballads
and calls it
In Memoriam
she'd seen the words
somewhere
but can't remember
where

falls asleep
in the tv's bluegreen glow
friends on either side
and stretched out
on the floor
limbs
touching
somehow all
connected
to each other
like spider strings
making
a fragile home

things she does the day of the wake

wakes up before
everyone else
peels herself out
from between blankets
and friends

walks upstairs
and hears
the stifled sobs behind
her mother's closed door
smells her stepfather's
cigarette

opens her brother's
bedroom door
not opened
since november

runs her fingers through
the dust on the dresser
the brush
still lying there
the blanket
her mother made him
when he was small
the glossy posters
sagging
their tape
drying

Katherena Vermette/95

epitaph

20 years later
they drive north
in the rain
she buys
one long
stemmed
red
rose
to lay at his grave

three hours up
the highway
7
68
17
talk about their lives
from their separate today
back to their
inseparable yesterday
women with
middle aged problems
girls with
big gulps

20 years later
his grave aged with tall weeds
still she knows exactly
where it is
walks through the soaked grass
as if called

she pulls the growth away
lays the long
red

rose
at the stone
she's never really liked
roses
and has no idea
if her brother ever did
but somehow
it reminds her of
long haired boys with
good intentions
and mischievous smiles

brothers annoying
and kind

lost little boys
just trying to find
their way
home

Katherena Vermette/97

I AM A NORTH END GIRL

verses in many voices

To see a World in a Grain of Sand
And a Heaven in a Wild Flower,
Hold Infinity in the palm of your hand
And Eternity in an hour.

—WILLIAM BLAKE

… and I've seen it all, everyone from my daughter to my grandmother struggle, scrimp and still barely have enough to save her soul

… I have been thrown out of the Northern at 1 am, 2 am, to lie like trash on the corner of Jarvis and Main waiting, just waiting for someone, something to haul me away

… I have left my kids to turn tricks at the corner, but I never go more than a block away, and always come back in the morning

… I have been hard up, strung up, beat up, held up but I can't seem to get high as often as I would like

… I am not cured, I am recovering; I am not a victim, I am a survivor

… and it's a war out there, people are dying, women are being raped, boys are getting killed, what else would you call it? All those guys, those that stick around, getting either shot or jail, or shot and jail, over and over and over

… I'm third generation welfare but first in my family to graduate, since residential schools anyways

… meth is the new crack was the new smack. I've been light years away for years and trust me, everyone likes it better that way

… and nobody cares nobody cares nobody cares and nobody is listening to what I have to say

… I have 4 kids by 3 different dads but this last one's been around for 2 years and he doesn't fight me and treats me right and I really, truly love him and believe, I think I even believe

… yeah I took him back I love him fuck you he loves me back better than anyone better than you got jealous bitch don't you worry about me I dish it out as much as I take it and I take it and dish it right back again and again don't you worry about that

… I have a good mom, a good dad, and didn't lose my virginity until I was 14 when some of my friends were already starting to have babies

… I'd do anything for my girls, my sisters, if they asked me to kill I'd get a gun and shoot 'til blood sprayed like rain, if they asked me to die, I'd lie down in the middle of Main and wait for some SUV to come blazing by and plow right over me. I'd do it for my sister girls 'cause I love them, 'cause they'd do it for me

… I have broken my wrist twice, cheek once, twisted my ankle a bunch of time trying to run away, and my collarbone's been cracked up so many times it just like pops out of place the moment I so much as flinch

… I have my life story in tattoos on my forearm, done up by Bobby with a broken bic pen and a blackened sewing needle

... I have a tumor on my cervix the size of a baseball
and smoke more than I should but I gave up drinking
3 years ago and never looked back

... it's not my fault, I can't, like, watch my kids 24/7

... and I have been doing it on my own for a long long
long time

... I am still here, lying in the ground, so close to the
highway I can still hear the cars, so close to the surface
I can still feel the sun, but I am dead, and I am red, and
they all stopped looking long ago

... I don't remember the last time I was touched in
either desire or kindness

... I don't know I don't know I don't know and if you
really want to know—I really don't ever want to find out

... when the night's been too long, when I get bored or
just mad and cold I run out into early morning traffic,
down by Aikins where those fucking white people are
going to their fucking jobs and I yell, "Hey you know
you want some of this!?" or something. The looks on
those faces, shit, you should see, it's fucking hilarious.
Have to get some attention some time fuck, they all
stopped noticing me there long ago

... my sister and I celebrate each full moon with a
drum circle and you know, I think the drum is actually
making me stronger

... we have victories too, the news just don't ever show them, but we do. Some of us, everyday is a victory— still alive victory. Survival—food clothing shelter food clothing shelter and then winter. Fuck—forget about doing anything else when there's fucking winter to deal with

... my grade six class is a lesson. A small microcosm of what the North End is. About twenty of us, late 1980s, so young. Now 4 of those guys are in jail, or just out, one's this big time pimp, more than half are still on welfare, most of the girls had babies before they were out of their teens, some of us just

... that old school is torn down now, but I still visit it in my dreams and it's always dusk and red and I am always speeding by in a car, stuck in the back seat and reving down the backlane. I see the boys in the schoolyard as I go by, they are playing ball against the bricks. I can hear the ball hit with that hollow sound. It echoes

... I have been wound up, worn out, spit on, knocked down

but I am still here

... and I am a role model

... I lived on Bannerman and Charles, Cathedral and MacGregor, Alfred and Arlington, in Jig Town awhile, but hell, I got out as quick as I could

... through and through and through, so nortend me

... can take the girl out of the nortend...

but I've never
not once
not for one second
looked away

Notes

Jeannette Winterson quote from *Why Be Happy When You Can Be Normal?* (Grove Press UK 2011)

Shohaku quote from haiku "The Cuckoo" translated by Henderson (late 17th or early 18th century) Found on: "Cool Bird Poems" by Tim Gannon, http://incolor.inebraska.com/tgannon/bird.html (a very good site for cool bird poems, go figure!)

e.e. cummings quote from the poem *i thank You God for most this amazing* (go to: http://ericwhitacre.com/blog/ e-e-cummings-reads-his-i-thank-you-god-for-most-this-amazing-day to hear the poet himself read it. So cool!!!)

Ursula K. Le Guin quote from *A Wizard of Earthsea* 1968

Skid Row quote from the song *I Remember You*, album *Skid Row* 1989

"mixed tape" song titles
18 and Life Skid Row *Skid Row* 1989
Patience Guns and Roses *G n R Lies* 1988
Long Cold Winter Cinderella *Long Cold Winter* 1988
Without You Motley Crue *Dr Feelgood* 1989
More than Words Extreme *Pornograffiti* 1990
Don't Know What You Got Cinderella *Long Cold Winter* 1988
Nothing Else Matters Metallica *The Black Album* 1991
Every Rose Has Its Thorn Poison *Open Up and Say... Ahhhh* 1988
What You Give Tesla *Psychotic Supper* 1991
Home Sweet Home Motley Crue *Theatre of Pain* 1985
Don't Cry Guns and Roses *Use Your Illusion I* 1991
November Rain Guns and Roses *Use Your Illusion I* 1991

William Blake quote from the poem *To See a World in a Grain of Sand* fragment from *Augeries of Innocence* "The Pickering Manuscript" 1803/1863

Acknowledgements

First, I have to thank the Canada Council of the Arts, Manitoba Arts Council and Winnipeg Arts Council, all of whom have given me money at one time or another. These organizations give indispensible, irreplaceable and oddly, invaluable support to artists everyday. Thank you.

Big thanks to Clarise Foster, my editor extraordinaire who managed to balance my many precarious selves.

All of my writing teachers along the way. I bring pieces of you with me.

The Aboriginal Writers Collective of Manitoba, without whom I'd be beers richer but all the poorer for it. Most especially, Dunc for the words, Rosie for leading the way, and Marvin for telling me my stuff was cool.

Ko'ona Cochrane who gave me the story of *cedar wax wing*.

Joanne Arnott for her gentle guidance and friendship.

Anna Lundberg for listening.

Adina Laskar for helping me to understand.

For my girls, Ela and Rowan, who never asked for a writer mom but have somehow managed the burden with grace and humour.

My lovely family, especially my mother, Eva Mohammed, and my father Pierre Vermette.

Reuben Boulette, for his art and other gifts.

Chrysta Swain Wood, my sister.

April Thomas, Jackie Pierson, and all the other beautiful nortendgrrls who stand in the periphery of these poems.

The North End, of course.

The River, despite our complicated relationship.

And Winnipeg, my love.

Versions of these poems have appeared in *CV2*, *Prairie Fire*, the MAWA Art Building Community Project 2008, *Canada and Beyond: A Journal of Canadian Literary and Cultural Studies*, and the anthologies, *A/Cross Section* (Manitoba Writers Guild 2007) and *Heute Sin Wir Hier/We Are Here Today* (Greifswald University 2009).